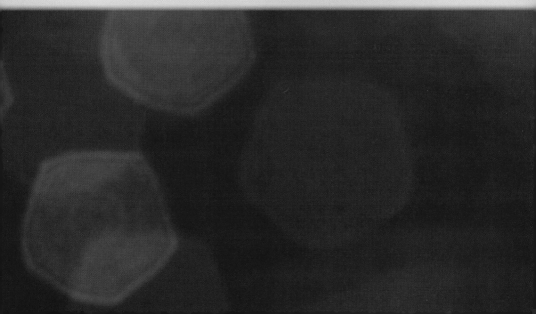

CONTEMPORARY LIVES

KEITH URBAN

AWARD-WINNING COUNTRY STAR

CONTEMPORARY LIVES

KEITH URBAN

AWARD-WINNING COUNTRY STAR

by Stephanie Watson

Essential Library

An Imprint of Abdo Publishing | www.abdopublishing.com

www.abdopublishing.com

Published by Abdo Publishing, a division of ABDO, PO Box 398166, Minneapolis, Minnesota 55439. Copyright © 2015 by Abdo Consulting Group, Inc. International copyrights reserved in all countries. No part of this book may be reproduced in any form without written permission from the publisher. Essential Library™ is a trademark and logo of Abdo Publishing.

Printed in the United States of America, North Mankato, Minnesota
092014
012015

THIS BOOK CONTAINS
RECYCLED MATERIALS

Cover Photo: Helga Esteb/Shutterstock Images
Interior Photos: Helga Esteb/Shutterstock Images, 3; Tammie Arroyo/
AP Images, 6–7, 32–33; Richard Drew/AP Images, 9, 98; Mark J. Terrill/
AP Images, 13, 59, 99 (top); Laura Farr/Zuma Press/Newscom, 14–15;
Warren Chan/Shutterstock Images, 17; Shutterstock Images, 20, 82, 96; Joe
Cavaretta/AP Images, 22; Jeff Christensen/AP Images, 24–25; Donn Jones/
Invision/AP Images, 30, 97 (top); Jason Moore/Zuma/Corbis, 39, 72; iPhoto
Inc./Newscom, 40; M. Spencer Green/AP Images, 42–43; Getty Images
Entertainment/Thinkstock, 45, 64, 97 (bottom); Reed Saxon/AP Images,
50; Mark Humphrey/AP Images, 52–53; Laura Farr/AdMedia/Newscom, 57;
Kathy Hutchins Photography/Newscom, 60–61; Tracey Nearmy/epa/Corbis,
67; Bob King/Corbis, 69; Steve Kohls/Brainerd Dispatch/AP Images, 74–75,
100; Khoi Ton/The Bulletin/AP Images, 78; Charles Sykes/AP Images, 84–85;
Grey Wasp/Blue Wasp/Splash News/Corbis, 88; Frank Micelotta/Invision for
FOX/AP Images, 91, 99 (bottom); Jack Plunkett/Invision/AP Images, 95

Editor: Mirella Miller
Series Designer: Emily Love

Library of Congress Control Number: 2014943856

Cataloging-in-Publication Data

Watson, Stephanie.
 Keith Urban: award-winning country star / Stephanie Watson.
   p. cm. -- (Contemporary lives)
Includes bibliographical references and index.
ISBN 978-1-62403-548-7
1. Urban, Keith, 1967- --Juvenile literature. 2. Country
musicians--Australia--Biography--Juvenile literature. 3. Singers--Australia--
Biography--Juvenile literature. 1. Title.
782.421642092--dc23
[B]

2014943856

CONTENTS

In the 2000s, Keith Urban was slowly gaining popularity in the country music industry after the release of his first album.

CHAPTER 1

Once in a Lifetime

||||||||||||||||||||||||||||||||||||||||||||||||

New York City isn't exactly the capital of country music. In fact, it is nearly 1,000 miles (1,600 km) away from the city that claims the right to that title—Nashville, Tennessee. Yet on the night of November 15, 2005, the Big Apple turned a little bit country.

On that night, Madison Square Garden—the city's famous arena in midtown Manhattan—was packed with musicians, producers, and fans. They were all there for the 2005 Country Music Association (CMA) Awards. Called "Country Music's Biggest Night," the CMA Awards are like the Oscars are to actors and actresses. Winning a CMA Award is proof a country music artist has made it in the industry.

One of the biggest awards at the CMAs is Entertainer of the Year. In years past, country legends including Garth Brooks, Shania Twain, Brooks & Dunn, and George Strait took home the bullet-shaped crystal trophy. In the 2005 ceremony, the nominees were equally impressive: Kenny Chesney, Alan Jackson, Toby Keith, and Brad Paisley. There was also a new name on the list. It was 38-year-old country-pop singer Keith Urban.

Though his first solo album had been released only a few years earlier, Urban was already getting a lot of attention in the industry. In 2000, the Academy of Country Music (ACM) had named him Top New Male Vocalist for his first solo album, self-titled *Keith Urban*. His 2002 follow-up album, *Golden Road*, had stayed on the country music chart for more than 100 weeks and had earned Urban a Grammy Award.

Urban also went on to win Male Vocalist of the Year at the 2005 CMA Awards for the second time.

Despite his successes, he knew he was in some pretty intimidating company at the CMA Awards. When presenter Shania Twain announced Urban was Entertainer of the Year, he was in total shock. Urban covered his face with his hands in disbelief as the crowd jumped to its feet and his song "Better Life" started playing over the loudspeaker. When Urban got to the podium, his first words were, "I'm completely weirded out at the moment."[1]

Urban thanked fellow nominee Kenny Chesney, with whom he had toured in 2003 as an opening act. He also thanked his mom, Marienne, who was in the audience clapping proudly for him.

It was a big moment for Keith Urban, and one that had taken decades of hard work and perseverance to achieve. He had grown up in Australia, a country not well known for its country music. Thanks to his musician father's influence, Urban had started listening to and playing country

"CAN I FRESHEN YOUR DRINK?"

Urban started from very humble beginnings. And he stayed humble, even when his songs began topping the charts and he was nominated for award after award. In 2004, when he won the CMA Award for Male Vocalist of the Year for the first time, Urban said, "I still somehow feel like I should be [carrying] a little hand towel and a tray, asking [the other nominees], 'Can I freshen your drink?'" It had taken him so long to reach the top he had a hard time believing his own success once he got there. "When I look at myself, I see the guy that's still struggling," he said.[2]

music when he was barely big enough to hold a guitar. He got his start onstage performing at festivals and talent shows—anywhere people would give him a chance to sing.

In those early years, Urban spent night after night playing in dingy roadhouse bars to a handful of people at a time. Yet he never gave up, because he knew writing and performing music was his dream—everything he wanted in his life. "It's like air to me, it's like breathing. It's just something that I not only want to do but I have to do," he said.[3] All the while, Urban had dreamed of moving to Nashville and making it big. But when he finally arrived there at age 25, he found the industry was not as accepting as he had hoped. The path to country stardom was steeper and rockier than he had expected.

Nashville record producers didn't take right away to Urban's unique blend of country, pop, and other musical influences. His Australian accent made him an oddity among the mostly southern- and Midwestern-born musicians and their country twangs. But once American audiences got a chance to listen to him, they fell in love with his sound and made Urban one of the biggest names in

URBAN STYLE

Urban has never been into the traditional garb many male country artists wear—button-down shirt, cowboy hat, and boots. He prefers a more casual look. His typical uniform is a T-shirt and a broken-in pair of jeans. He believes clothes should be comfortable. "I don't suffer for fashion," he said. "If you don't feel comfortable, then the clothes wear you."[4]

country music. Not bad for a guy who was born halfway around the world from Nashville, in the little town of Whangarei, New Zealand.

It took Urban nearly a decade to get his first solo album produced and on the charts.

Urban performed in 2001 as part of Brooks & Dunn's tour.

CHAPTER 2

Worlds Away

Whangarei, New Zealand, is worlds away from the bright lights and twanging guitars of Nashville, Tennessee. It's more than an 8,000-mile (13,000 km) journey from the United States' country music mecca. Whangarei is New Zealand's northernmost city, located approximately 100 miles (160 km) from the capital of Auckland.

It was in this coastal region that Keith Lionel Urban was born on

October 26, 1967. He was welcomed into the world by his parents, Robert (Bob) and Marienne Urban, and his older brother, Shane. Bob and Marienne were New Zealand natives. Both had grown up on farms there.

When Keith was young, Bob and Marienne decided to move their family to another country

KEITH'S HOMETOWNS

The coastal New Zealand city where Keith was born is called Whangarei. Its name means a gathering place either for whales or for chiefs, depending on the interpretation. Either way, the name fits. Whales gather in Whangarei's harbor during the summer months to feed, and tribal chiefs were in charge there during its early years. Whangarei's landscape is lush and dramatic. Visitors who explore the area find steep hillsides, palm tree–fringed beaches, and the soaring rise of long-extinct volcanoes. The city's central feature is its harbor, which was formed when massive ice sheets melted during the last Ice Age.

The town Urban considers his true home is Caboolture, which sits about an hour's drive north of Brisbane on the eastern coast of Australia. Caboolture is home to the Kabi—a group of Aboriginals, the native people of Australia. The name Caboolture comes from the Kabi word meaning "Place of the Carpet Snake." Europeans first settled the town in the early 1840s. Today, Caboolture has a vibrant tourist community and hosts an annual country music festival.

Though Keith wasn't born in Caboolture, he considers it his hometown.

and start a new life. They traveled nearly 1,400 miles (2,300 km) with their two young boys to Brisbane. This city on the eastern coast of Australia is the capital of the province of Queensland. Eventually, they settled in the farming community of Caboolture, just a few miles to the north of Brisbane.

The Urban family had a small farm of its own, as well as a convenience store. They were every bit the working-class family. When he was young, Keith worked on the farm. He collected eggs from the hens, milked the cows, and cleaned out the pigsty. But he did not always do a good job.

It was quickly apparent that farming wasn't his life's calling.

In those early days, Keith learned a lot from watching his parents. He picked up his resourcefulness from them. He learned he could get a lot accomplished without a lot of money. He also learned about the importance of finding the perfect partner in life. He explained,

> It's easy to cut and run from family problems, but [my parents have] persevered and really are the best of friends. They love being together. I'm grateful to have that example; I grew up seeing what a marriage can be, and that it can be long and lasting.[1]

A MUSICIAN IS BORN

Keith also inherited a love of country music from his father, who had played drums in a band back in the 1950s. Keith would spend hours listening to his dad's albums from US country legends Glen Campbell, Don Williams, Ronnie Milsap, and Charley Pride. From very early on, Keith knew exactly where he was headed. "On the back of

COUNTRY MUSIC IN AUSTRALIA

Australia has long had its own thriving country music scene. It started in the 1800s, when settlers from other countries brought their banjos, harmonicas, and stories of struggle and strife to Australia. The man known as the father of Australian country music was Tex Morton (born Robert William Lane in New Zealand), who started recording in the 1930s. He combined the US country music style with local folk stories to create a uniquely Australian sound. Artists such as Slim Dusty and Buddy Williams helped to popularize country music in Australia during the 1940s, 1950s, and 1960s.

all the records it would always say, 'Recorded in Nashville, Tennessee.' So as a kid I just thought, 'That's where you go to make records. And when I'm old enough to get there, I'll get there,'" he said.[2]

When Keith was just four years old, his dad bought him a ukulele, which he strummed along with the radio. Two years later, his parents promoted him to his first guitar. They got him lessons by making a deal with a local music teacher. She could advertise her business by putting a sign in their store window, as long as she was willing to teach their son how to play guitar. She agreed, and pretty quickly Keith took

Urban taught himself guitar by mimicking songs he heard on the radio.

to plucking and strumming its strings. By the time he was seven, he had already competed in his first talent show.

"For me, playing guitar and singing was just like walking. One day you start walking, and you never question it, and you just keep walking for the rest of your life," he said.[3] Keith eventually grew to dislike his guitar teacher, but he continued teaching himself how to play on his own.

The sound that would one day make Keith famous—a blend of classic country and modern pop—can be traced all the way back to age six or seven, when he bought his first pop album. "Right there between the country music my dad played and my love of commercial, hooky songs was the foundation of my music," he said.[4]

Keith performed whenever and wherever he could. He joined a guitar group that did shows at retirement homes. He also signed up for the Westfield Super Juniors, a local talent act that performed musicals. He acted and danced in them, too. By the time Keith was eight years old, his parents had become part of the Northern

JOHNNY CASH LIVE IN BRISBANE

By the early 1970s, Johnny Cash was already an icon in US country music. His 1968 album, *Johnny Cash at Folsom Prison*, had gone gold and earned him two Grammy Awards. As part of a 1973 tour, Cash played in Australia. He stopped for one performance at Brisbane Festival Hall. In the audience was a very excited little boy named Keith Urban, who was wearing the western shirt and bolo tie his father had bought him for the occasion. "I remember the roar of the crowd and then this you-can-hear-a-pin-drop silence when he sang. It was electrifying," Keith remembered many years later.[5]

Urban's star power has been obvious since he was a child.

Suburbs Country Music Club. It was one of several groups around Australia that would gather regularly to share their love of country music. Once a month, Keith would get up onstage with the house band at these get-togethers and sing. Country music clubs from different parts of Australia would often compete with one another at festivals. Soon, Keith was also taking part in these festivals, performing songs by US country artists such as Charlie Pride, Tanya Tucker, and Dolly Parton.

Keith felt right at home onstage in front of an audience. In fact, the stage was one of the few places where the shy nine-year-old felt totally comfortable. "I loved it so much because it was the place where I could be more of the person I wished I could be, 'cause I was intrinsically shy and quiet," he said.[6]

Even as a kid, Keith seemed to have the makings of a star. Australian country music radio broadcaster Nick Erby did an interview with Keith in 1981. "He was quiet, yet confident and had a definite aura about him even then," Erby recalled.[7] It would not be long before Keith's personality would blossom even more on a much bigger stage.

FIRE!

When Keith was ten years old, a fire destroyed his family's home. Friends in the community immediately came to their aid. They gave the Urbans a place to live, and a local country music club held a fund-raiser to help them rebuild. "Country music came to the rescue immediately," Keith said. From the experience, he learned the importance of giving back to others. Today he lends his talents to many charity events, explaining, "When those opportunities come, it's a no-brainer to me. I know what it's like to lose things."[8]

Urban was a natural performer in front of large audiences.

CHAPTER 3

Future Plans

||||||||||||||||||||||||||||||||||||||||||||||||||||||||||||||||||||||||||||||||||

As a teenager, Keith wanted to spend all of his time focusing on his music. The trouble was, he still had to devote most of that time to being a student. "The only thing stopping me playing four or five nights a week was having to get up for school," he said.[1] As a singer and guitarist, he was a natural. In the classroom, he struggled. He couldn't wait to get out of school and on with his musical career.

By age 14, Keith had developed enough of his own musical style to put together his first band. It was called California Suite. They performed US rock tunes by bands such as the Eagles and Fleetwood Mac.

According to Australian law, kids have to stay in school until they are at least 15. As soon as his fifteenth birthday passed, Keith dropped out of high school and was on to new things. His parents knew he was following his heart. "Music was always his passion," his mother said.[2]

A MUSICAL EPIPHANY

Keith listened to many musicians for inspiration. But one of the pivotal moments in his musical career came in 1988, when he saw John Cougar Mellencamp perform in Australia as part of his Lonesome Jubilee Tour. On the *Lonesome Jubilee* album, Mellencamp added a lot of folk and country sounds, blending fiddle, accordion, and acoustic and electric guitars. "It was the closest thing to a musical epiphany," Keith says of hearing the songs.[3] "It changed my whole world. I couldn't decide if I was going to do rock or country. Then along comes *Lonesome Jubilee*. . . . What I heard was that you could blend all your influences. That's what John really inspired me to do."[4]

FRACTURED MIRROR

Keith's musical roots were in country music, but by the time he was 15, he was into an edgier sound. Heavy metal, with its ripping guitars and screaming intensity, matched his new teen angst. A friend asked Keith to play guitar in his metal band, Fractured Mirror. They played cover tunes of 1980s metal acts such as Judas Priest, the Scorpions, and Black Sabbath. The trouble was that Keith was still a little too country to fit in. "So, we're playing like a Judas Priest song, and they'd throw me the solo, and I'm like 'Su-wah-tikka-tikka,' all this chicken pickin' guitar pro," he said.[6] His time with Fractured Mirror was short-lived. The band fired him after only one week.

After quitting school, Keith started playing in a band five nights a week, just as he had wanted. The band performed at little clubs and bars around Brisbane. Although he was leading a very adult life, Keith wasn't able to forget that he was still just a teen. "I couldn't drive until I was 17, so Mom and Dad had to drive me to all my gigs!" he said. "They'd sit patiently and wait for the show to be over and then drive me home."[5]

CALIFORNIA SUITE

Keith continued developing his musical style by listening to different pop, rock, and country artists. He was a big fan of guitarists Mark Knopfler of the rock band Dire Straits, Lindsey Buckingham of Fleetwood Mac, and Ray Flacke, an English country musician.

In 1983, when Keith was 16 years old, the Country Capital Music Association (CCMA), a community-based country music group in Australia, named him its Junior Male Vocalist. That same year, Brisbane club owner Greg Shaw was looking for a new house band when he caught a performance by California Suite. As soon as he saw

TALENT SHOW

Keith appeared in a number of talent shows as a teen, and he won a few of them. In 1983, at age 16, he appeared on the Australian television talent show *New Faces*. Wearing a red and white pantsuit, his shaggy blond hair falling over its wide collar, Keith strummed his guitar and sang the romantic ballad "All Out of Love" by the Australian band Air Supply. The judges weren't easy on Keith. They told him he had potential, but they said his voice still wasn't mature enough and he needed more practice.

Keith perform, Shaw knew he'd found a star. "I really want to manage him," Shaw later recalled.[7]

Yet Shaw knew Keith wasn't quite mature enough musically to stand in the spotlight on his own. So he teamed him up with a popular Queensland band he was managing, Rusty & The Ayers Rockettes. At first, Keith was put in charge of the band's lighting. While setting up the lights, he watched Rusty & The Ayers Rockettes and learned how to play all of their songs, which were cover versions of popular country tunes. When their guitar player, Brad Hooper, left the band in 1988, Keith took over for him.

Although Keith was part of a popular band, he wasn't content playing cover songs. After a year, he decided to leave the band.

|||||||||||||||||||||||||||||||||||||||||||||||||||||||||||||

ON TO SOMETHING NEW

Urban formed his own band, which gave him the chance to perform some of the original songs he'd been writing. Then in 1990 came a pivotal moment in his career. Urban entered Star Maker—Australia's top talent competition for country singers. He won.

Urban spent time in the recording studio writing and recording songs for his first album.

Urban's win gave him the chance to catch the attention of EMI record company in Australia. They signed the 23-year-old to a record deal. Under EMI, he released his first solo album, self-titled *Keith Urban*. Urban wrote most of the songs on the album, including the first single, "Got It Bad." He also wrote the tracks "Future Plans" and "Hold On to Your Dreams." The titles could have described Urban's own musical aspirations.

The album's songs backed up country lyrics with electric guitars. *Keith Urban* produced four hits in Australia. The song "I Never Work on a Sunday" also earned Urban a 1991 Golden Guitar—Australia's country music award—for New Talent of the Year. The same album earned him two Golden Guitars the following year, for Male Vocalist of the Year and Instrumental of the Year. Urban was making a name for himself in his home country. But still, he wanted more. He yearned to be in the country music capital of the world—Nashville, Tennessee.

|||||||||||

KEITH'S BELOVED GUITAR

In 1989, Urban traveled from Australia to New York City on his first trip to the United States. While there, he visited Manny's Music, a legendary music store in Times Square. In a glass case, Urban spotted a rare fortieth anniversary Fender Telecaster. The guitar company made only 300 of these guitars.[8] "I remember walking in and it was like . . . this Holy Grail of a guitar for me," Urban recalls.[9] The guitar cost approximately $2,500—a fortune to him at the time. By borrowing money from friends and digging through his own savings, he managed to scrape together enough to buy the guitar. He named it Clarence, after the angel in the movie *It's a Wonderful Life*. He used it to record his very first album, and the guitar has stayed with him for more than two decades.

With Urban's move to the United States, he became an unknown in the country music industry.

CHAPTER 4

Headed for a
Better Life

||||||||||||||||||||||||||||||||||||||||||||||||||||||||||||||||

U rban had scored four country hits, along with three major music awards in his native country. Still, he wasn't satisfied. He wanted to make a name for himself in the United States.

Urban's manager, Greg Shaw, was able to get him into the United States on an extraordinary alien visa. This travel document lets foreigners stay in the

THE EAGLE

IIIIIIIIIIIIIIIIIIIIIIIIIIIIIIIIIIIIIIIIIIIIIIIIIIIIIIIIIIIIIIIIIIIIIIIIIIIIIIIIIIIIIIIIIIIIIIIIIIIIIIII

Urban has collected a few tattoos over the years. His very first one was of an eagle, which sits proudly on his right shoulder blade. He got it when he was 25 years old and had just arrived in the United States. The eagle has since been joined by a phoenix on his left forearm and the word "love" on his left shoulder blade. He's inked his wife Nicole Kidman's name on his right bicep, and her initials on one wrist. And Urban has a sun tattoo on his chest for his older daughter, Sunday Rose.

country for one year or more because they have a special talent in science, education, business, or the arts.

In 1992, at age 25, Urban finally arrived in Nashville, the city he'd been dreaming about since childhood. With that move, he went from one of the top artists in his home country to a total unknown. Yet he did not mind the drop in status.

For the next five years, Urban struggled to make a name for himself in his adopted country. He didn't yet have a record deal, so he had to make do on what little money he could earn writing songs for other artists.

IIIIIIIIIIIIIIIIIIIIIIIIIIIIIIIIIIIIIIIIIIIIIIIIIIIIIIIIIII

34 | CONTEMPORARY LIVES: KEITH URBAN

THE RANCH

Urban also played gigs at clubs and bars with his band, which he brought with him from Australia was made up of two other members. Jerry Flowers played bass guitar and sang backup, and Peter Clarke took the drums. The three musicians moved into a crumbling old house in Nashville. They mowed lawns and did other odd jobs to earn enough money to keep their band afloat and take them from gig to gig.

Eventually Urban got a deal with Warner Brothers to record an album, but the deal was just for him. Warner Brothers wanted a solo artist. He went into the studio with many different producers

AN AUSSIE IN NASHVILLE

In Australia, people in the music industry had been honest with Urban about his potential. In the United States, everyone told him he was great and then nothing happened for him. This confused Urban. Then there was the accent. Urban was living in the center of country music, where everyone talked with a southern twang. With his strong Australian accent, Urban really stood out. He even surprised a few folks. "At meet-and-greets, I'd shock the little kids," he says. "A 4-year-old would hear me talk and say, 'Oh my God! He's a Wiggle!'"[1] The Wiggles are a group of Australian children's performers.

and backup musicians, but the record would not come together. "It all sounded like karaoke to me. I couldn't find my voice in the studio," he recalled.[2] Finally, he asked if he could use his own band on the album.

Under the name the Ranch, Urban's band recorded song after song for Warner Brothers. The record label still was not happy. It was a difficult time for Urban and his fellow bandmates. "It just seemed like nothing [my band and I] did was connecting or happening and it was very frustrating," he says.[3] Out of the 12 songs the Ranch recorded for their self-titled debut record, Warner's executives did not think there was a single hit. But fortunately, someone else did.

> "Signing Keith was a no-brainer. He is a world-class guitarist and entertainer. It just seemed like it was only a matter of time before it all came together for him as an artist."[4]
>
> –SCOTT HENDRICKS ON SIGNING KEITH URBAN

In 1997, Scott Hendricks, president and CEO of Capitol Records Nashville, listened to the Ranch's record. He liked it enough to sign Urban and his band to a record deal.

Yet the album didn't propel Urban into the US country music scene as he had hoped. Although critics praised *The Ranch*, the record company didn't promote it enough, which meant consumers didn't buy it. The album flopped. Urban was at a crossroads. He had to decide what his next move would be.

||||||||||||||||||||||||||||||||||||||||||||||||||||||||||||||

BREAKUP

A period of poor health would ultimately decide Urban and his band's fate. Urban developed problems with his vocal cords and was forced to take approximately one year off from singing. With their lead singer out of commission and the band going nowhere, in 1998, the Ranch broke up.

After the Ranch disbanded, Urban played guitar for big country bands, including the Dixie Chicks and Brooks & Dunn. He even played on Garth Brooks's *Double Live* album, which went double platinum, selling more than 2 million copies in its first three weeks.[5]

WHAT HAPPENED TO THE RANCH?

After the Ranch broke up in 1998, Urban became a mega country star. But what happened to his bandmates, Jerry Flowers and Peter Clarke? Flowers went on to perform with the Dixie Chicks. He has also played guitar and sang with other country artists, including John Berry and Gary Allan. In 2006, he reunited with Urban to sing backup vocals for his *Love, Pain & the Whole Crazy Thing* album. Clarke returned to Australia, where he continues to perform.

But playing behind the scenes for other artists was no longer enough for Urban. He missed his family back home in Australia, and he was depressed about his stalled career. "Not being able to play for months at a time was really hard," he said.[6] "Everything went wrong, and I went through a black period in my life."[7]

During that dark time, Urban looked to drugs and alcohol for solace. He started drinking heavily and using cocaine. His addiction spiraled out of control. "I remember one night crawling around on my hands and knees, looking for these little rocks [of cocaine] at five in the morning, and I was drenched in sweat. It was the worst," he later recalled.[8]

After Urban's band broke up, he played guitar for many other famous country singers.

Urban knew if he was going to have
any chance at a country music
career, he needed to get clean.

YOU'RE NOT MY GOD

Cocaine had such a strong hold on Urban in the late 1990s he called his addiction "demonic."[9] He wrote a song about overcoming addiction, called "You're Not My God," which appeared on his 2002 *Golden Road* album. In the song, he expressed his anger at the drugs that controlled him for a time:

"You're not the truth/
You're a temporary shot/
You ruin people's lives and you don't give a second thought"[10]

Urban checked himself in at the Cumberland Heights alcohol and drug treatment center in Nashville. Although he quit rehab just a few weeks later, he kept working toward sobriety on his own. He relied on his spirituality and his music to help him stop using drugs.

By 2001, Urban's popularity in the United States was quickly growing.

CHAPTER 5
Out on His Own

After the Ranch's album failed and the band broke up, Urban went his own way. This time his record company, Capitol, gave him the freedom to do what he wanted. So he started work on a solo album.

Keith Urban, self-titled like the album he had put out years before in Australia, was released in 1999. It features a mix of upbeat pop-country blends like "It's a Love Thing," along with "Where the

Blacktop Ends" and other more traditional country tracks. Urban also added a few romantic ballads, including "Your Everything" and "You're the Only One." He wrote many of the songs himself. The experience of writing for this album was different than it had been when he was with the Ranch. "The songs were more personal," he said. "It didn't feel like a band record this time around."[1]

It took some time for the album to gain traction. But in early 2001, the single "But for the Grace of God" reached Number 1 on the US country charts. Urban had his first big hit in the states.

Country radio stations quickly fell in love with the Australian country star. "He's the best guitarist I've ever heard, and his voice is incredible," said Debby Turpin, assistant program director at KSOP, a country music station in Salt Lake City, Utah.[2] "He makes our job easier," said Kerry Wolfe, director of programming for FM 106.1 in Milwaukee, Wisconsin. "He's unique because he appeals to both males and females. The guys dig him for his ability to thrash a guitar like no other, and his live shows are electric."[3]

Urban's guitar skills were
one reason fans loved
seeing Urban play live.

Urban received a huge honor for his album at the ACM Awards, when he was named 2000's Top New Male Vocalist. Urban accepted his award by thanking country radio, God, and his mother.

URBAN ROMANCE

In 1992, when Urban had still been struggling to find his place in the Nashville country music scene and make a hit record, he met a veterinary technician named Laura Sigler. In 2001, Urban thought he was ready to settle down with Sigler. He decided to declare his love in a pretty dramatic way, by hiring a man to stand outside a Nashville restaurant holding a sign that read "Will You Marry Me?"

The proposal was unforgettable, but in 2002, Urban and Sigler split up. She later said of her former fiancé, "Keith is charming and very charismatic, but not reliable."[5] Getting over Sigler was hard, but Urban turned to songwriting to help him heal. He wrote about Sigler in the song "Somebody Like You," which he put on his next album, *Golden Road*. "When you put your arms around me, you let me know there's nothing in this world I can't do," the song goes.[6]

Strangely enough, Urban met the woman who would soon become his next "somebody" when she appeared in the video for "Somebody Like You."

THE FRISBEE DOG MOMENT

Urban has had a few epiphanies over the years. One is an experience he now calls the "Frisbee Dog Moment." After playing a show in Australia, Urban hung out with some old childhood friends. A few of them were married and still living in the area where they had all grown up. Urban felt bad for them because they had never seen the world as he had. But his old friends felt bad for *him*. They thought it was sad that Urban was spending most of his life on a tour bus, with no wife and no roots.

When Urban came back home to Nashville, he was playing Frisbee with his dog in his backyard one day. Suddenly, he realized he wanted all the same things his friends had—the marriage and stability. He just wasn't ready to settle down yet. "I needed to figure that out, and that was the start of things starting to work in my life," he said.[7]

Supermodel Niki Taylor and Urban hit it off right away. They both shared a love of country music. Taylor showed her affection by nicknaming Urban "Kiki." She also got a tattoo on her right arm to match one her new boyfriend had. It read, *Amor Vincit Omnia*, which is Latin for "love conquers all."

Urban and Taylor dated on and off for approximately two years, until 2004. Eventually, their careers got in the way and they broke up. Yet the breakup wasn't bitter, and the two stayed friends afterward. Both Urban and Taylor have since had their matching tattoos removed.

|||||||||||||||||||||||||||||||||||||||||||||||||||||||||||

GOLDEN ROAD

"Somebody Like You" was one of the songs Urban wrote for his *Golden Road* album, which was released in October 2002. The title of the album represents taking the right road in life—one that Urban has not always followed. "I was on [the right road] for a long time. Then I took some really bad detours and dead ends. Now, I feel like I'm back on track," he said.[8]

LEARNING TO APPRECIATE DAD

All of the songs were deeply personal for him. One of them, called "Song for Dad," was a tribute to his father back in Australia. He used the lyrics of the song to thank his dad for "how much he loved my mother and my brother and me."[9]

The album spawned four hits on the *Billboard* country chart. Three of them reached Number 1: "Somebody Like You," "Who Wouldn't Wanna Be Me?," and "You'll Think of Me," which also crossed over and climbed the pop music charts.

Clay Hunnicutt, who was regional vice president of programming for Clear Channel radio stations in the southeast, said Urban had "the complete package—looks, style and the music to go with it." He predicted the singer was "one of the top candidates for the next level

Golden Road stayed on the country chart for more than 100 weeks and earned Urban his first Grammy Award.

When an artist puts out a new album, he or she promotes it by touring the country doing concerts. In the summer of 2003, Urban went out on the road as part of Kenny Chesney's Margaritas and Señoritas Tour. Urban was Chesney's opening act. Being on the road meant living on a tour bus, keeping up a hectic pace, and rarely going home. But that suited Urban just fine. "There's an energy you have to achieve to be on the road, and when you come home, you don't want to decompress and lose it all. You want to maintain that energy, you want to get back out there," he said.[12]

of superstardom."[11] Hunnicutt knew what he was talking about. Superstardom was just around the corner.

Urban wrote most of the songs on his third album, *Be Here*.

CHAPTER 6

Good Thing

||||||||||||||||||||||||||||||||||||||||||||||||||||||||||||||||||||||||||

I n the summer of 2004, Urban's career was on a roll. He had sold millions of albums and had hit the Number 1 spot on the charts four times with his first two records, *Keith Urban* and *Golden Road*.

In September 2004, in the middle of his meteoric rise to fame, Urban released his third solo album, titled *Be Here*. A few songs he cowrote with other artists, including 1980s pop singer Richard Marx ("Better Life") and country songwriter Monty Powell ("Days Go By"). He said the song "Days Go By" really captured the theme of the whole album. "It's the passing of time and how fast it goes," he said. "I don't want to miss any of this right now. It's a really good time."[1]

Once again Urban had a hit record on his hands. The singles "Making Memories of Us" and "Better Life" spent 11 weeks on top of the *Billboard* country chart in 2005.[2] The album was such a big deal that Urban's record label, Capitol, considered him as big an artist as Garth Brooks.

MOVING BACKWARD

With the release of the album *Be Here*, Urban's career was going in fast-forward. But in his video for the single "Days Go By," he briefly went in the opposite direction. During one scene in the video, Urban walks forward down a city street while people rush around him in reverse. It is a cool effect, but one that was not easy for Urban to pull off. During the video shoot everyone else walked forward, while Urban had to sing while walking backward, an unusual challenge. Then the director ran the whole scene in reverse.

BE HERE—THE TOUR

To support the album, Urban embarked on a national tour. Though he had toured before, it was only as an opening act for other country artists. This would be his first time taking the stage as a headliner since he had arrived in Nashville 12 years earlier.

The Be Here '04 Tour launched October 8, 2004, in Muncie, Indiana. From there Urban and his band set off on a string of performances in 20 cities, including Dallas, Texas; New York City, New York; Milwaukee, Wisconsin; and Cleveland, Ohio. Making the jump from opening act to headliner was a big change for Urban. "We're on buses versus crammed into a van, and people are showing up versus not showing up," he said. "And they know your songs!"[3] Headlining on tour was also a good way to earn a living, Urban was discovering. He earned nearly $11 million from concerts alone in 2005, according to *Billboard* Boxscore. And he ranked seventh on the list of the top earning country artists that year.

Yet playing in a different city every night for many weeks in a row was not as exciting and

AN ORGANIC ROCK BAND

Back in the late 1980s, Urban had learned from John Mellencamp that musicians don't have to stick with the instruments that are expected for their kind of music. As a country artist, Urban could expand beyond banjos and twangy guitars. So on his own records and tours, Urban started playing around with different instruments. He blended accordions, fiddles, and acoustic guitars to create a new kind of sound.

glamorous as it might seem. The endless tour bus legs and nights away from home took their toll on Urban.

MORE AWARDS

With the *Be Here* album came more recognition from the country music industry. Urban was nominated for four CMA Awards in 2005. He took home two, Entertainer of the Year and Male Vocalist of the Year.

Urban's influence was also spreading outside of country music. On February 8, 2006, Urban took home his first Grammy Award, for Best Male Country Vocal Performance. On the Grammy

Urban's music had a wide appeal and was played on pop and adult contemporary radio stations, as well as country stations.

THE REAL KEITH URBAN ‖‖‖

Audiences get to know musicians by reading the interviews they give to reporters, listening to their music, and watching them perform onstage. Yet it can be hard for the public to really get to know any big star—especially one like Urban, who works very hard to keep his personal life private. Urban's former manager, Anastasia Brown, offered some insight into the tight-lipped star's personality. "He's extremely intense," Brown said. "He's got a wicked sense of humor. It can be dry and take you off-guard. You wonder what he's going to say next."[4]

Awards show, Urban performed "You'll Think of Me," the song that won him the award.

Everything seemed to be coming together for Urban. He was churning out hits and earning millions of dollars. The music industry was giving him one big award after another. Yet one thing was missing. After two failed relationships, Urban was alone. Though women screamed for him night after night at his concerts, there was no one waiting for him when he got home. A chance meeting would change that and introduce Urban to the love of his life.

‖‖‖‖‖‖‖‖‖‖‖

Urban celebrates with the audience after his performance at the 2006 Grammy Awards.

Urban arrives at the
2005 G'Day LA event.

CHAPTER 7

Homespun Love

O n January 15, 2005, Urban was honored at G'Day LA in Los Angeles. The annual G'Day events showcase famous Australians who have made an impact in the arts, movies, fashion, and business around the world. Other honorees that night included actor Mel Gibson and Oscar-winning actress Nicole Kidman.

Before the ceremony, Urban attended an event for the honorees. At one point, he looked across the room and saw

Nicole Kidman. He was entranced and more than a little intimidated by the willowy blonde actress. "I swear to you, she glided across the room, like floated. I don't know how she did it. It's like she's standing there, and she didn't walk. It was out of this world," he recalled.[1]

Urban finally got up the nerve to go up to Kidman and introduce himself. The two talked for a while. Then, as the conversation wound down, he got the distinct feeling that he was bothering Kidman, so he said it was nice to meet her and went on his way. He went over to a friend, who pointed out that maybe Kidman wasn't bothered and really did want to keep talking to him. So Urban went back over and apologized to her for leaving. They started talking again, and hit it off right away.

Even though there was an obvious attraction between the musician and the actress, it took Urban four months to finally ask Kidman out on a date. It wasn't an easy time for either of them. Urban had already been through two failed long-term relationships. Plus, he was constantly out on the road touring to promote his albums. Kidman was busy with her movie career. She also was scarred from the difficult divorce she had gone through with actor Tom Cruise in 2001. She came out of that marriage afraid she would never find love again. But after meeting Urban, she was so moved by him she prayed for some divine intervention. "I remember thinking, Oh, my God, if you ever gave me a man like that, I promise I would be completely devoted for the rest of my life," she said.[2]

"Definitely we both met each other exactly at the right time. She said early on that she wanted to be brave with me. I felt there was something else at work, bringing us together and then just continuing to watch over us."[3]

–KEITH URBAN ON HIS RELATIONSHIP WITH NICOLE KIDMAN

It was obvious something really big was brewing between the two of them. Urban called it a "divine coming together."[4]

Nicole Kidman and Urban began quietly seeing each other in 2005.

FALLING IN LOVE

Rumors started flying about the couple when they began appearing in public together. In August 2005, they were spotted riding a motorcycle and having lunch at a health food restaurant in Woodstock, New York. Kidman was shooting a movie in New York City at the time. When reporters asked if the two were dating, Urban's media representative insisted they were just friends.

Yet people who knew them painted a different picture. "They were inseparable," a friend of Urban's told reporters. "It was obvious something is there—a lot more than just a friends situation."[5] Kidman showed up at many of the stops on Urban's 2005 tour. She would jump up and down and scream along with his songs, just like a fan.

KIDMAN GETS A LITTLE BIT COUNTRY

When Kidman and Urban first started dating, Kidman did not know much about country music. So Urban thought he would give his new girlfriend a little education. He brought her to Nashville and took her to a record store, where he bought her a CD by legendary country artist Waylon Jennings. In the car on their way home, Urban put on the song "Are You Sure Hank Done It This Way" to see her reaction. She was hooked. "I hit play and the minute that bass drum started and the guitar started she said, 'Oh I like this, turn this up!'" Urban said. "We turned it up as loud as the stereo would allow in the car and she instantly fell in love with this song and I believe from there country music."[6]

In November 2005, she flew her parents from Australia to spend Thanksgiving with Urban and his parents at his Nashville home. In February, she accompanied him to the Grammy Awards ceremony, where he won the Best Male Country Vocal Performance award for "You'll Think of Me." At around that time, photographers spotted Kidman wearing a diamond ring on her ring finger. The media was abuzz, wondering if the two were engaged.

WEDDING BELLS

As it turns out, they were engaged. On June 25, 2006, Urban, 38, and Kidman, 39, made their love official. They were married inside the stone Cardinal Cerretti Memorial Chapel near Sydney, Australia, where Kidman had grown up. As she drove to the church in the back of a white vintage Rolls Royce, people lined the streets of Sydney, cheering for her. The display of affection from her fans brought her to tears.

More than 200 guests awaited her inside the old stone chapel, where 1,000 candles flickered. It looked like a fairy tale. An organist played

Kidman arrives at the chapel for her wedding to Urban.

"Bridal Chorus" by the German composer Wagner
as Kidman walked down the aisle accompanied
by her father, Antony. She wore an ivory silk
chiffon gown created by French designer Nicolas
Ghesquière for Balenciaga. Her sister Antonia was
maid of honor. Isabella, her 13-year-old adopted

daughter with Tom Cruise, was a bridesmaid. Urban's brother, Shane, was best man.

When Kidman arrived at the altar, Urban was waiting for her, beaming. They looked at each other, "and it was like it was just the two of them in their own little world," one guest said.[7] The Kidman family priest, Father Paul Coleman, married them. After the "I do's," Urban and Kidman shared what one guest called "the longest, most passionate kiss."[8] Everyone cheered.

After walking down the aisle for the first time as a couple—and getting showered with rose petals along the way—the couple and their guests moved to a tent set up outdoors for the reception. Everything inside was red, from the roses to the carpet. The event was lavish, costing the couple an estimated $250,000. Approximately one-third of that money was spent on party favors, including engraved Tiffany clocks that were given to every guest.

Urban's father gave an emotional toast to the new couple. As befitting a musician's wedding, there was also plenty of music. Australian actor Hugh Jackman sang. So did Neil Finn, a fellow

Kidman and Urban threw an
extravagant party for all of their
wedding guests.

Kidman and Urban are popular in both Hollywood and Nashville circles, and their wedding guest list proved it. A number of famous faces were in attendance, including Kidman's fellow Australian actors Hugh Jackman, Russell Crowe, and Naomi Watts. Australian media mogul Richard Murdoch was also there. So was Capitol Records Nashville president Mike Dungan.

New Zealander who was lead singer of the 1980s band Crowded House. Urban serenaded his new bride with his song "Making Memories of Us," which brought her to tears.

The newlyweds spent the night at the Park Hyatt Sydney. The following afternoon, they took off for a very exotic and private honeymoon at the Saint Regis Resort in Bora Bora, French Polynesia.

|||||||||||||||||||||||||||||||||||||||||||||||||||||||||||

LOVE, PAIN & THE WHOLE CRAZY THING

Urban and Kidman had the storybook wedding and what seemed like the perfect love. But eventually they had to get back to work. In the fall of 2006, Urban released his next album, *Love,*

Pain & the Whole Crazy Thing. He expressed his devotion for his new bride in songs such as "Got It Right This Time" and "Won't Let You Down." In "Once in a Lifetime" he sings about his hope for their future together. "It's a long shot, baby, I know it's true. But if anyone can make it, I'm bettin' on me and you."[9] Along with the love songs and slower ballads, Urban stayed true to his pop and rock roots by adding a few upbeat tunes to the album, such as "Faster Car" and "I Told You So."

Critics gave *Love, Pain & the Whole Crazy Thing* mixed reviews. One reviewer called it a combination of "artistic efforts" and "Nashville

"STUPID BOY"

Urban writes many of his songs himself. But sometimes he also covers songs from other artists. For his album *Love, Pain & the Whole Crazy Thing*, he chose a song called "Stupid Boy," written by singer-songwriter Sarah Buxton. In the song, Buxton expresses her anger to a man who has stolen her friend's dreams and destroyed her life. Urban loved the lyrics, but he realized he couldn't sing "Stupid Boy" as if he were saying those words to another man. He asked Kidman, who had a solution. "No, you're looking in the mirror, singing this song," she said.[10] "Stupid Boy," with its sad, haunting lyrics, earned Urban a Grammy Award for Best Male Country Vocal Performance.

After his wedding, Urban quickly got back to work releasing new music.

pop-chart fodder."[11] A critic from *Slant* magazine said it was "self-indulgent and over-produced," although he did admit that Urban is a "phenomenal guitarist."[12] Yet fans loved it. The first single off the album, "Once in a Lifetime," became the highest-debuting single in the entire history of the *Billboard* Hot Country Songs chart.

Everything seemed to be going Urban's way. He was living out the "love" part of his album title with his new wife. Yet the "pain" that had chased him during his early days in Nashville was not far away. It was about to make a very unwelcome return to his life.

||||||||||

Urban took time in 2006 and 2007 to attend treatment for his drug and alcohol addictions.

CHAPTER 8

The Hard Way

ust four months after Urban's fairytale wedding to Kidman, as he was releasing his new album, *Love, Pain & the Whole Crazy Thing,* and getting ready to launch the tour to support it, everything came crashing down. On October 19, 2006, he suddenly canceled his tour and checked himself in at the Betty Ford Center, a drug and alcohol abuse treatment center near Palm Springs, California.

The cocaine addiction that had brought Urban to his knees in the late 1990s was back.

Urban released a statement in which he apologized to his family, friends, and wife. "I deeply regret the hurt this has caused Nicole and the ones that love and support me," he wrote.[1] But instead of running away from her new husband's problems, Kidman stood firmly by his side. "I've learned an enormous amount having a relationship with someone who is in recovery," she said. "I'm more than willing to walk it with him."[2]

Kidman, along with some of Urban's friends, staged the intervention that helped get him into rehab. He went along willingly. He knew if he didn't do something to stop using drugs, he'd lose everything he loved. "I had to make a decision which road I was going to take, once and for all," he said. "I'd been at that crossroads before and always taken the wrong road."[3] Urban was inspired by his wife's devotion, which he said made him want to be a better man.

Friends also stood by Urban during his difficult recovery. "He's a strong and amazing person," said his former manager, Anastasia Brown.

Urban is not the only celebrity to struggle with addiction—or the only one to get sober at the Betty Ford Center. *Iron Man* star Robert Downey Jr. checked in for 67 days in 1998. Actress Lindsay Lohan went there to get clean in 2013. And rocker Ozzy Osbourne stayed there in 1984. Former First Lady Betty Ford started the California-based center in 1982 after going through her own recovery from alcohol addiction. Today, the Betty Ford Center offers alcohol and drug treatment programs for men, women, and children. People can live at the center for 30 to 90 days—however long it takes them to get well.

"So he's dealing with this challenge just as he does with everything in life—with grace, strength, and integrity."[4] In January 2007, 90 days after he had entered the Betty Ford program, Urban checked out, finally free from drugs and alcohol.

|||||||||||||||||||||||||||||||||||||||||||||||||||||||||

BACK ON THE ROAD

That summer, Urban finally hit the road for the Love, Pain and the Whole Crazy World Tour he had postponed to go into rehab. The tour launched June 8 in Phoenix, Arizona. It took him from coast to coast—California to Pennsylvania, Wisconsin

Urban performs in Connecticut in 2007 as part of the Love, Pain and the Whole Crazy World Tour.

to Washington, DC, and just about everywhere in between.

He was glad to be back on tour, and grateful to his wife for helping him get back to his life and career. At one show, he told the 15,000 fans in attendance, "I would not be here tonight playing for you guys if it wasn't for the extraordinary faith and love of my wife."[5] He dedicated his song "Got It Right This Time" to her.

It was hard for Urban to be away from Kidman while he was on the road. Sometimes he would take a break from his concerts and travel to visit her on the set of whatever movie she was filming at the time. To keep her close when he had to be far from her for long stretches of time, Urban would watch Kidman's movies on television. For every night he was away, he would leave Kidman a love letter to remind her how much she meant to him.

|||||||||||||||||||||||||||||||||||||||||||||||||||||||||

A SPECIAL KIND OF LOVE ||||||||||||||||||||||||||||||||||||||||||||||||||

Urban and Kidman have made no secret about how much they love each other. "I really feel like I was just sort of lost until I found Nic," Urban has said. "She's really been life-giving for me. I wasn't able to give myself to anybody until I met her." He praises her "loving heart" and "great sense of humor."[6] Kidman calls Urban her "great love" and says they are "very, very close."[7]

SETTING UP ROOTS
IN NASHVILLE

Nashville had been Urban's home since the early
1990s. Now he needed to find a place where
he and his wife could set up house together. In
2007, the couple bought a 36-acre (15 ha) farm
near Leipers Fork, Tennessee, a town 30 minutes
southwest of Nashville. It was about as far from the
bright lights of Hollywood as Kidman could get,
but that suited her just fine. "I have a real desire
to be outdoors, a desire for simplicity—a slightly
slower, relaxed approach to life. A community,
not a big-city feel. That's what I grew up with, and
it's what I prefer," she said.[8] Urban also loved the
Nashville area, and he had no plans to leave it.

It wasn't long before they were regular
fixtures at the local coffee shop, supermarket,
and gym. They were such regulars at one café,
Bread & Company, they became known as the
"oatmeal-and-egg-white-omelette couple"—the
dishes they ordered every time they came in. They
fit right in to the down-to-earth community.

Urban and Kidman feel right at home at their Leipers Fork estate, but it is not their only home. So the pair can also stay tied to their Australian roots and visit friends and family from time to time, they bought a mansion in the southern highlands of New South Wales, Australia. On the mansion's grounds, they raise cattle and alpacas. Urban says that while he loves the South, he still thinks like an Australian.

AND SUNDAY ROSE MAKES THREE

Once they were settled in their new home, Urban and Kidman could focus on starting a family together. Kidman already had two adopted children with former husband Tom Cruise—Connor and Isabella. They chose to live in Los Angeles with Cruise. Urban was happy to play stepdad to his wife's two children, but he and Kidman wanted to have children together.

Yet Kidman was nervous. She had two miscarriages while married to Cruise, and she wasn't sure she'd ever give birth to her own child. In January 2008, Kidman, at age 40, announced she was pregnant. The couple was thrilled. "When I first saw the baby on the ultrasound, I started

Kidman and Urban announced they were pregnant with their first child in 2008.

crying," Kidman said. "I didn't think I'd get to experience that in my lifetime."[9]

On July 7, 2008, Kidman gave birth at a Nashville hospital. Urban was by her side. The couple's daughter, Sunday Rose Kidman Urban, was born weighing 6 pounds, 7.5 ounces (2.9 kg). She was named after Sunday Reed, a well-known patron of the arts in Victoria, Australia. Nicole was "euphoric" about her new daughter, said a friend. Urban said "There was a new feeling of loving what I did, a new joy, a new sense of purpose."[10]

He wrote about his gratitude to his wife and new daughter in the liner notes of his 2010 album, *Get Closer*. "Nicole Mary—I continue to be brought to my knees by this love of ours. . . . I am in awe of how this blessed family we are creating stretches and fearlessly opens my vulnerable heart . . . and I just want to be a better man, for you, and father for our heavenly Sunday Rose."[11]

A THOUSAND-YEAR FLOOD

Just as Urban was starting to record his seventh studio album, *Get Closer*, a catastrophic meteorological event struck Tennessee. Between May 1 and 2, 2010, more than 13 inches (33 cm) of rain fell on the Nashville area. The Cumberland River overflowed into the city. Water spilled over the river's banks, flooding downtown homes and businesses. The rush of water was so extreme it was termed a 1,000-year flood. The country music capital was hit hard. The Grand Ole Opry House was left underwater. So was SoundCheck, a facility where musicians store their instruments and rehearse. Fifty of Urban's guitars were there, and many were ruined. Urban was fortunate that he had the money to replace what he had lost in the flood. Many other people in the area weren't so lucky. Nearly 11,000 homes and businesses were destroyed or damaged.[12] Urban helped out by appearing on the "Flood Relief with Vince Gill & Friends" and "Music City Keep on Playin'" telethons, which raised money for flood victims.

Even with his busy schedule, Urban has made it a rule never to be away from his family for more than three days at a time.

CHAPTER 9

Sweet Things

||||||||||||||||||||||||||||||||||||||||||||||||||||||||||||||||||||||||||||||||||||

There were more albums and more tours ahead. But this time, Urban was not going on the road for long stretches of time alone and coming back to an empty house. He had his wife and daughter to come home to. Sometimes his family would come with him on his tour bus so they could all be together.

Urban returned from touring for long enough to write his 2009 album, *Defying Gravity*, from the family's Tennessee home. He would sit in a downstairs room, watching deer outside as he wrote the songs by hand in a notebook. As always, the songs reflected his life at the time—especially the emotions he felt for his family. "Being a husband and a father influences everything. I've written about longing, hope, loss. . . . It all takes on a new meaning because of my family," he said.[1]

Because the focus of his life was on his wife and daughter, many of the songs were about love. He penned "Why's It Feel So Long" one morning, ten minutes after Kidman had left for the airport and he already missed her. "Time keeps dragging on til you get back home," he wrote.[2] In another track on the album, "If I Could Ever Love," he describes how love turned his life around.

The lyrics and music also connected with fans. *Defying Gravity* debuted at Number 1 on the *Billboard* top 200—the first of his albums to reach that mark so quickly. The album also earned him his third Grammy Award—Best Male Country Vocal Performance for the song "Sweet Thing."

URBAN'S NEED FOR SPEED

Being a busy musician and father doesn't leave much time for hobbies. But one of Urban's great loves—other than his music and family—is his car and motorcycle collection. One of his first automotive splurges was on a Chevy Impala SS, for which he paid $21,000 using his very first music royalty check. He later added to his collection a Bentley—a British luxury car—and several motorcycles, including a Harley Davidson Fat Boy One-Hundredth Anniversary edition, which was a gift from Kenny Chesney.

HAVE A LITTLE FAITH

In mid-January 2011, Urban and Kidman announced they had welcomed another daughter into their lives on December 28, 2010. This came as a huge surprise to fans and the media, because Kidman had never appeared pregnant. It turned out the baby, Faith Margaret, had been born to a surrogate—a woman who had carried the couple's biological child in her own womb.

They had turned to a surrogate because Kidman had so much trouble getting pregnant and carrying babies in the past. Kidman thought of Sunday Rose as her "miracle," and she was not sure she could give birth to another baby. She and Urban decided

Urban takes his daughters to a park in Sydney, Australia.

to keep the surrogacy a secret until after their baby was born.

The couple chose the name Faith because they needed to have faith they could have another child. Margaret was for Kidman's grandmother, who gave birth to her last child at age 49. "As an older mother I wanted to pay tribute to her," said Kidman, who was 43 when Faith was born.[3]

Urban stepped easily into the role of dad with both his girls. He took them to the park to play and he sang with them. He also gave them piggyback rides around the house. "I get Sunday on my back, and I get Faith on Sunday's back, and I hang on to them, and off we go down the stairs," he said.[4]

Aside from the fact that mom often went off to shoot movies, and dad had to record albums and tour, the family's life was pretty normal. Urban

A FAMILY FULL OF SINGERS

Urban isn't the only one with vocal talent in his family. His wife is also a good singer. Kidman sang in the 2001 movie *Moulin Rouge* with Ewan McGregor. She performed a duet with Urban at a 2010 G'Day event in Los Angeles. They sang together at a children's hospital in 2014 as well. Daughter Sunday is also a bit of a crooner. She loves to sing songs such as "I Love It" by Icona Pop and "I Gotta Move My Jacket," her version of "Moves Like Jagger" by Maroon 5. While Urban was finishing an album, he took Sunday to the studio and pressed record on the machine. He told her to say "Hi," but instead she sang "Twinkle Twinkle Little Star."

and Kidman would take the girls to school in the mornings. They went to the grocery store and movies together. "Family is definitely a priority in Nashville. And that fits us perfectly," Urban said.[5]

|||||||||||||||||||||||||||||||||||||||||||||||||||||

AMERICAN IDOL

In September 2012, Urban embarked on a new career venture. He was chosen to be one of the new judges on season 12 of the hit talent show *American Idol*. Urban was slated to sit on the panel along with pop diva Mariah Carey and rapper Nicki Minaj, as well as longtime *Idol* judge Randy Jackson. Although Urban's managers would not reveal how much he was making, Minaj reportedly earned $12 million for the one-year deal, and Carey pocketed just under $18 million.

Urban remembered from his own talent show days what it was like to perform onstage in front of judges, and he vowed to be truthful but not mean to the *Idol* contestants. Though he had high hopes for his turn at judging *Idol*, season 12 was disappointing. A feud erupted between rival divas Minaj and Carey. Ratings for the show were the lowest they had ever been. The future of *American*

Urban jokes around with Lopez and Connick during a press panel for *American Idol*.

Idol seemed to be up in the air. *Idol*'s future became even more uncertain when Minaj, Carey, and Jackson all announced they would not be coming back for the next season.

Yet Urban was still in. He returned in January 2014 to judge season 13 of *American Idol*, along with Jennifer Lopez (who had been on the panel during seasons 10 and 11) and crooner Harry Connick Jr. Right away the trio seemed to be a

When season 13 of *American Idol* premiered in January 2014, the media could not help but notice a chemistry blooming between two of its judges. It wasn't between Jennifer Lopez and Keith Urban or Harry Connick Jr. Instead, it was Connick and Urban who seemed to be in perfect tune with one another. Their easy rapport led some members of the media to speculate about whether a "bromance" was brewing between the two men. Urban and Connick, who are the same age, admitted they hit it off right away. Urban said, "We have a mutual respect—and we really like each other!"[7] "Keith and I both love puns and wordplay," added Connick. "We are always trying to have some one-upmanship."[8]

good fit. "It's just fluid, it's very easy to do," Urban said of working with Lopez and Connick. "To use a dancing metaphor, they're great dance partners."[6]

FUTURE PLANS

It had taken Urban a long time to find his groove—in music, in life, and in love. But in 2014, at age 46, he had finally achieved a kind of contentment.

In September 2013, he released his eighth studio album, *Fuse*. He launched the 58-city Light the Fuse Tour—which included stops in his native Australia—to promote the album. Urban's new music earned him even more ACM nominations, including ones for Male Vocalist of the Year and Video of the Year for "Highway Don't Care," a song he recorded with Tim McGraw and Taylor Swift.

The following spring he told reporters he was back on board for season 14 of *American Idol*. He was also planning the Raise 'Em Up Tour for the summer of 2014. Along with recording and performing music, Urban launched a fragrance and his own line of T-shirts. And he was constantly

URBAN'S OTHER VENTURES |||||||||||||||||||||||||||||||||||||||||||

Music is Urban's main passion, but he has also tried his hand at other business ventures, including fragrance and fashion. In 2011, he launched Phoenix, a cologne for men. He said the scent was inspired by his father's taste in cologne. In 2014, he started his own line of T-shirts, By Keith Urban. "I've always loved cool, interesting T-shirts and wanted to share that passion, but only if I could do it in a fun, collaborative way—with social impact that can help make a difference," he wrote on the T-shirt line's website.[9] Urban's shirts feature spiritual and universal themes—such as a map of the world, a mandala (the Hindu symbol of the universe), and a mystic seahorse with wings. His company promises to reinvest the money it earns into local communities.

thinking of new and different career avenues to explore. "Just within music, there's a myriad of things I'd like to do," he said.[10]

One of those things was to help others. Urban has lent his name, and his talents, to many charities over the years. He and Kidman are on the advisory board of Artists for Peace and Justice, which promotes peace, social justice, and poverty relief around the world. He has performed at fund-raisers to benefit organizations such as Habitat for Humanity and the Country Music Hall of Fame. And he's created an affordable line of guitars, the URBAN Guitar Collection, to help aspiring musicians.

Even in the midst of his constantly changing and often hectic schedule, Urban never forgets what is most important to him. He tries to spend as much time as possible with his family. "Somewhere in the last couple of years, I've really grasped the concept of the brevity of time," he said. "It's very, very fleeting. No matter how many years are ahead of us, it will all be gone very quickly. I don't want to miss any of it."[11]

||||||||||

Urban continues to grow as a musician and family man.

TIMELINE

1967

1983

1983

Keith Urban is born on October 26 in Whangarei, New Zealand.

The Country Capital Music Association (CCMA) in Australia names Keith best Junior Male Vocalist.

At age 16, Keith appears on the Australian TV talent show *New Faces*.

1990

1991

1992

Urban wins Star Maker, Australia's talent competition for country singers.

Urban wins a Golden Guitar—Australia's country music award—for New Talent of the Year.

At age 25, Urban arrives in Nashville.

Urban joins Rusty & The Ayers Rockettes, a popular Queensland, Australia, band.

Urban sees John Cougar Mellencamp perform in Australia and learns music can include all different kinds of influences.

Urban travels from Australia to New York City on his first trip to the United States.

Capitol Records signs Urban and his band, the Ranch, to a record deal.

Urban wins Top New Male Vocalist at the ACM Awards.

Urban proposes to girlfriend Laura Sigler.

TIMELINE

2003

2004

2005

Urban is the opening act for Kenny Chesney's Margaritas and Señoritas Tour.

Urban launches his Be Here '04 tour, which is his first time as a headlining act.

Urban wins the CMA Entertainer of the Year and Male Vocalist of the Year Awards.

2006

2007

2008

Urban checks himself in at the Betty Ford Center, a California drug and alcohol abuse treatment center, for cocaine and alcohol abuse.

Kidman and Urban buy a 36-acre (15 ha) farm near Nashville, Tennessee.

Kidman gives birth to the couple's first child, Sunday Rose, on July 7.

2005

Urban and Nicole Kidman meet at the G'Day LA event honoring Australians in Los Angeles.

2006

Urban takes home his first Grammy Award for Best Male Country Vocal Performance.

2006

Urban and Kidman get married in Sydney, Australia, on June 25.

2010

Their second daughter, Faith Margaret, is born via a surrogate on December 28.

2012

Urban joins the judging panel on the hit TV show *American Idol*.

2013

Urban releases his eighth studio album, *Fuse*.

FULL NAME

Keith Lionel Urban

DATE OF BIRTH

October 26, 1967

PLACE OF BIRTH

Whangarei, New Zealand

MARRIAGE

Nicole Kidman (June 25, 2006–)

CHILDREN

Sunday Rose (born July 7, 2008)

Faith Margaret (born December 28, 2010, via surrogate)

ALBUMS

Keith Urban (1991), *The Ranch* (1997), *Keith Urban* (1999), *Golden Road* (2002), *Be Here* (2004), *Love, Pain & the Whole Crazy Thing* (2006), *Greatest Hits* (2007), *Defying Gravity* (2009), *Get Closer* (2010), *The Story So Far* (2012), *Fuse* (2013)

TELEVISION APPEARANCES

American Idol

SELECTED AWARDS

- Won CMA Entertainer of the Year and Male Vocalist of the Year Awards in 2005.
- Won first Grammy Award for Best Male Country Vocal Performance in 2006.
- "Once in a Lifetime," off the album *Love, Pain & The Whole Crazy Thing,* becomes the highest-debuting single in the history of the *Billboard* Hot Country Songs chart.

PHILANTHROPY

Keith Urban has performed at benefits, donated songs, and done other work to support a number of charities over the years, including: Artists for Peace and Justice, Habitat for Humanity, URBAN Guitar Collection, and telethons.

> "I can be exhausted or sick as a dog, or going through something in my life, but every single time I walk onstage and see the audience, it's unbelievable. There's always this euphoric energy."
>
> —KEITH URBAN ON THE POWER OF MUSIC

GLOSSARY

angst—A feeling of worry or anxiety.

aspiration—A dream or hope of achieving something great.

Billboard—A music chart system used by the music recording industry to measure record popularity and sales.

brevity—The shortness of time.

debut—A first appearance.

epiphany—An experience in which someone suddenly comes to a new realization.

euphoria—A feeling of great excitement.

Grammy Award—One of several awards the National Academy of Recording Arts and Sciences presents each year to honor musical achievement.

intervention—An action taken to prevent someone from hurting themselves; for example, trying to stop someone from taking drugs or alcohol.

intimidate—To make someone afraid.

intrinsic—Part of the nature of something or someone.

liner notes—Information about a record, CD, or tape that is printed on its cover or on a piece of paper placed inside its cover.

mecca—A place that has a certain significance to a group of people.

phoenix—A magical bird in ancient stories that lives for 500 years before it burns itself to death and then is born again from the ashes.

platinum—A certification by the Recording Industry Association of America that an album has sold more than 1 million copies.

self-indulgence—The gratification of one's own desires, passions, or whims.

single—An individual song that is distributed on its own over the radio and other mediums.

solace—Comfort during a difficult time.

twang—A sharp, nasal tone.

willowy—Gracefully tall and thin.

SELECTED BIBLIOGRAPHY

John, Elton. "Keith Urban." *Interview.* October 2006: 135–136. Print.

Keeps, David A. "Urban Legend." *Best Life.* Dec/Jan 2007: 96–103. Print.

"Keith Urban Biography." *People.* People.com, n.d. Web. 15 April 2014.

Leonard, Elizabeth. "Keith Urban 'I Was Going to Lose It All.'" *People.* 12 Nov. 2007: 68–73. Print.

Roland, Tom. "Urban Cowboy." *Billboard.* 13 Nov. 2010: 18–21. Print.

FURTHER READINGS

Apter, Jeff. *Fortunate Son: The Unlikely Rise of Keith Urban.* Sydney: Random, 2011. Print.

Bertholf, Bret. *The Long Gone Lonesome History of Country Music.* New York: Little, 2007. Print.

Hamen, Susan E. *Australia.* Minneapolis: Abdo, 2013. Print.

WEBSITES

To learn more about Contemporary Lives, visit **booklinks.abdopublishing.com**. These links are routinely monitored and updated to provide the most current information available.

PLACES TO VISIT

Grammy Museum
800 W. Olympic Boulevard
Los Angeles, CA 90015
http://www.grammymuseum.org
213-765-6800
This museum in downtown Los Angeles has exhibits on four floors that cover many aspects of musical history including technology, the creative process, and the history of the Grammy Awards.

Music City Walk of Fame
4th Avenue South
Nashville, TN 37203
http://www.visitmusiccity.com/walkoffame/default.htm
Music City Walk of Fame honors artists who lived, worked, and played in Nashville with a sidewalk star. Keith Urban was honored in May 2011.

Urban Country Music Festival
Caboolture, Queensland, Australia
http://www.urbancountry.com.au/default.aspx
1-800-810-400
Experience Caboolture's largest country music festival in the city Keith Urban refers to as his hometown. Despite the festival's name, it is not named after Urban, but rather celebrating country and urban lifestyles.

SOURCE NOTES

CHAPTER 1. ONCE IN A LIFETIME

1. "Keith Urban Won Entertainer of the Year 2005 CMA Awards." *YouTube.com*. YouTube, 9 Sept. 2011. Web. 23 July 2014.

2. Phyllis Stark. "Keith Urban." *Billboard* 25 Sept. 2004: 13, 63. Print.

3. "Keith Urban–The Road To Be Here." *YouTube.com*. YouTube, 20 Jan 2013. Web. 19 May 2014.

4. InStyle staff. "Keith Urban to InStyle: "I Don't Suffer for Fashion." *InStyle.com*. Time Inc., 24 June 2013. Web. 23 July 2014.

CHAPTER 2. WORLDS AWAY

1. David A. Keeps. "Urban Legend." *Best Life* Dec./Jan. 2007: 96–103. Print.

2. John Mellencamp. "Keith Urban." *Interview* 1 Aug. 2006: 123. Print.

3. Danielle Anderson. "I Count My Blessings Featuring Keith Urban." *People* 5 Dec. 2013: 42–44. Print.

4. "On the Record Keith Urban." *People* Nov. 2013: 28. Print.

5. Ibid.

6. Elizabeth Leonard. "Keith Urban 'I Was Going to Lose it All.'" *People* 12 Nov. 2007: 68–73. Print.

7. "Urban Legend." *Capital News*. Country Music Capital News, Jan. 2006. Web. 23 July 2014.

8. Tom Roland. "Urban Cowboy." *Billboard* 13 Nov. 2010: 18–21. Print.

CHAPTER 3. FUTURE PLANS

1. David A. Keeps. "Urban Legend." *Best Life* Dec./Jan. 2007: 96–103. Print.

2. Jason Lynch and Chris Strauss. "Country Loving." *People* 10 Apr. 2006: 100–103. Print.

3. "On the Record Keith Urban." *People* Nov. 2013: 28. Print.

4. Zac Childs. "Keith Urban: Down-Under Uber-Picker." *VintageGuitar.com*. Vintage Guitar, Inc., March 2007. Web. 23 July 2014.

5. Danielle Anderson. "I Count My Blessings Featuring Keith Urban." *People* 5 Dec. 2013: 42–44. Print.

6. Conan O'Brien. "Keith Urban Played with the Rolling Stones." *TeamCoco.com*. Team Coco Digital LLC, 7 May 2013. Web. 23 July 2013.

7. "Urban Legend." *Capital News*. Country Music Capital News, Jan. 2006. Web. 23 July 2014.

8. "Custom Shop 40th Anniversary Telecaster 1989 Collectors Edition." *GaryDavies.com*. Gary Davies, n.d. Web. 1 May 2014.

9. "Keith Urban on the Telecaster, Part 1." *YouTube.com*. YouTube, n.d. Web. 1 May 2014.

CHAPTER 4. HEADED FOR A BETTER LIFE

1. "Keith Urban." *People* 15 Nov. 2004: 80. Print.

2. Zac Childs. "Keith Urban: Down-Under Uber-Picker." *VintageGuitar.com*. Vintage Guitar, Inc., March 2007. Web. 23 July 2014.

3. Elizabeth Leonard. "Keith Urban 'I Was Going to Lose it All.'" *People* 12 Nov. 2007: 68–73. Print.

4. "Scott Hendricks Biography." *Scotthendricks.info*. Scott Hendricks, n.d. Web. 23 July 2014.

5. Randy Reiss. "Garth Brooks Goes Double Platinum in Third Week." *MTV.com*. MTV News, 10 Dec. 1998. Web. 5 May 2014.

6. David A. Keeps. "Urban Legend." *Best Life* Dec./Jan. 2007: 96–103. Print.

7. Deborah Evans Price. "Aussie Keith Urban Debuts on Capitol." *Billboard* 25 Sept. 1999: 43. Print.

8. "Urban to Fight Off Addiction." *Theage.com.au*. Fairfax Digital, 23 Oct. 2006. Web. 23 July 2014.

9. Karen S. Schneider, et al. "A Sobering Decision." *People* 6 Nov. 2006: 48–51. Print.

10. "You're Not My God." *AZlyrics.com*. AZLyrics.com, n.d. Web. 23 July 2014.

CHAPTER 5. OUT ON HIS OWN

1. Deborah Evans Price. "Aussie Keith Urban Debuts on Capitol." *Billboard* 25 Sept. 1999: 43. Print.

2. Ibid.

3. Tom Roland. "Urban Cowboy." *Billboard* 13 Nov. 2010: 18–21. Print.

4. Danielle Anderson. "I Count My Blessings Featuring Keith Urban." *People* 5 Dec. 2013: 42–44. Print.

5. Caroline Graham. "The Wedding's Off, Nicole Tells Urban Cowboy." *MailOnline*. Daily Mail, 22 Jan. 2006. Web. 8 May 2014.

6. "Somebody Like You." *AZlyrics.com*. AZLyrics.com, n.d. Web. 23 July 2014.

7. David A. Keeps. "Urban Legend." *Best Life* Dec./Jan. 2007: 96–103. Print.

8. M. B. Roberts. "Keith Urban: Road Less Traveled 2002." *Countryweekly.com*. American Media, Inc., 28 Aug. 2012. Web. 23 July 2014.

9. Ibid.

10. Ibid.

11. Phyllis Stark. "Keith Urban." *Billboard* 25 Sept. 2004: 13, 63. Print.

12. Country Weekly Staff. "From the Vault: Keith Urban (2003)." *Countryweekly.com*. American Media, Inc., 13 Jan. 2011. Web. 8 May 2014.

CHAPTER 6. GOOD THING

1. "Keith Urban, Be Here Interview CMTNews." *YouTube.com*. YouTube, 1 Feb. 2012. Web. 19 May 2014.

2. Ken Tucker. "6 Questions with Keith Urban." *Billboard* 11 Mar. 2006: 48. Print.

3. "Keith Urban." *People* 15 Nov. 2004: 80. Print.

4. Jason Lynch and Chris Strauss. "Country Loving." *People* 10 Apr. 2006: 100–103. Print.

CHAPTER 7. HOMESPUN LOVE

1. WENN. "Keith Urban—Urban Cut Short First Kidman Meeting." *Contactmusic.com*. Contactmusic.com, 30 Nov. 2010. Web. 23 July 2014.

2. "Nicole Kidman: 'I Prayed To God' After Meeting Keith Urban." *Huffingtonpost.com*. TheHuffingtonPost.com, 5 Jan. 2011. Web. 23 July 2014.

3. Elizabeth Leonard. "Keith Urban 'I Was Going to Lose it All.'" *People* 12 Nov. 2007: 68–73. Print.

4. Ibid.

5. "Nicole Kidman, Keith Urban: Engaged?" *People.com*. Time Inc., 16 Nov. 2005. Web. 23 July 2014.

6. Erin Duvall. "Keith Urban Convinces Nicole Kidman to Hank-Up the Radio." *Theboot.com*. Taste of Country Network, 16 Nov. 2010. Web. 23 July 2014.

7. Michelle Tauber, et al. "Nicole and Keith's Magic Night." *People* 10 July 2006: 58–63. Print.

8. Ibid.

9. "Once In A Lifetime." *AZLyrics.com*. AZLyrics.com, n.d. Web. 23 July 2014.

10. Elton John. "Keith Urban." *Interview* Oct. 2006: 135–136. Print.

11. Ted Drozdowski. "Keith Urban: Love, Pain and the Whole Crazy Thing." *ThePhoenix.com*. Phoenix Media, 20 Nov. 2006. Web. 23 July 2014.

12. Jonathan Keefe. "Keith Urban: Love, Pain & The Whole Crazy Thing." *Slantmagazine.com*. Slant Magazine, 27 Nov 2006. Web. 22 May 2014.

CHAPTER 8. THE HARD WAY

1. Tamara Conniff, Ray Waddell, and Ken Tucker. "Urban Developments." *Billboard* 11 Nov. 2006: 32–34. Print.

2. Elizabeth Leonard. "Keith Urban 'I Was Going to Lose it All.'" *People* 12 Nov. 2007: 68–73. Print.

3. US Weekly Staff. "Keith Urban Thought Rehab Would 'Destroy' Nicole Kidman Marriage." *USMagazine.com*. US Weekly, 29 Nov. 2010. Web. 23 July 2014.

4. Karen S. Schneider, et al. "A Sobering Decision." *People* 6 Nov. 2006: 48–51. Print.

5. Elizabeth Leonard. "Keith Urban 'I Was Going to Lose it All.'" *People* 12 Nov. 2007: 68–73. Print.

6. Danielle Anderson. "I Count My Blessings Featuring Keith Urban." *People* 5 Dec. 2013: 42–44. Print.

7. Luchina Fisher. "Nicole Kidman on Husband Keith Urban: 'I've Met My Great Love.'" *ABCNews.go.com*. ABC News Internet Ventures, 29 Oct. 2013. Web. 23 July 2014.

8. "'I'm a Country Girl at Heart': Nicole on Turning Her Back on the Bright Lights of Hollywood for Quiet Life in Nashville." *DailyMail.co.uk*. Associated Newspapers, 11 Feb. 2014. Web. 23 July 2014.

9. Michelle Tauber, et al. "Nicole & Keith's BABY BLISS!" *People* 21 July 2008: 62–66. Print.

10. Eileen Finan. "Behind the Lyrics." *People* 10 March 2010: 30. Print.

11. Danielle Nussbaum. "Keith Urban." *InStyle* July 2013: 56–57. Print.

12. "May 2010 Flood: By the Numbers." *The Tennessean*. Gannett, 1 May 2011. Web. 12 Aug. 2014.

CHAPTER 9. SWEET THINGS

1. Danielle Anderson. "I Count My Blessings Featuring Keith Urban." *People* 5 Dec. 2013: 42–44. Print.

2. "Why's It Feel So Long." *AZLyrics.com*. AZLyrics.com, n.d. Web. 23 July 2014.

3. Baz Bamigboye and Sara Nathan. "Surprise! Surrogate Baby Joy for Nicole Kidman and Keith Urban as They Welcome Faith to the Family." *DailyMail.co.uk*. Associated Newspapers, 18 Jan. 2011. Web. 23 July 2014.

4. Danielle Anderson. "I Count My Blessings Featuring Keith Urban." *People* 5 Dec. 2013: 42–44. Print.

5. Julie Jordan. "Country's Hottest Guys." *People* 4 May 2011: 42. Print.

6. Gerri Miller. "How Does Keith Urban Describe His Marriage to Nicole Kidman?" *YourTango.com*. Tango Media Corporation, n.d. Web. 23 July 2014.

7. Patrick Gomez. "Harry & Keith: The Music Men." *People* 7 Apr. 2014: 82. Print.

8. Ibid.

9. "By Keith Urban." *ByKeithUrban.com* n.d. Web. 26 May 2014.

10. Elizabeth Leonard. "Keith Urban 'I Was Going to Lose it All.'" *People* 12 Nov. 2007: 68–73. Print.

11. Danielle Anderson. "I Count My Blessings Featuring Keith Urban." *People* 5 Dec. 2013: 42–44. Print.

ABOUT THE AUTHOR

Stephanie Watson is a freelance writer and editor based in Rhode Island. Over her 20-plus-year career, she has written for television, radio, the Web, and print. Stephanie has authored more than 24 books, including *Celebrity Biographies: Daniel Radcliffe, Elvis Presley: Rock & Roll's King*, and *Cee Lo Green: Rapper, Singer, & Record Producer*.